The Usborne
Classical Music
Picture Book

Anthony Marks

Illustrated by Galia Bernstein
Designed by Jamie Ball

Contents

Throughout this book you'll see QR codes, like this one. These are links to listen to music samples on a smartphone or tablet. You can find out more at the back of this book.

Don't worry if you don't have a smartphone or tablet – you can listen to the music samples at the Usborne Quicklinks website, and you'll find links to websites to find out more about classical music there too.

What is classical music?

People have been making all kinds of different music for
thousands of years – to sing and dance to, to pray,
or to show off political or military power.

In ancient Roman times,
musicians played in
parades to celebrate
military victories.

This 15th-century painting by Dutch artist Hans Memling shows angels
singing and playing music to God.

In 1717, Handel wrote
Water Music for King
George I, who wanted an
evening concert on the River
Thames. The King was
accompanied by musicians in
barges, followed by dozens
of other boats.

Musical pageants on water, like this one painted by Italian artist Giovanni Antonio Canal,
known as Canaletto, were a popular way for a monarch to show off pomp and power.

Writing music down

Before sound recording was invented just over a
hundred years ago, a lot of music was lost forever as
soon as it was sung or played. But some of it didn't
get lost, because it was written down. This is what
most people think of as classical music.

People who invent music and write
it down for other people to play
are known as composers.

The first music writing

People first began inventing ways of
writing music down thousands
of years ago – in order to help
them remember and share
it. This eventually
developed into
the system we
use today.

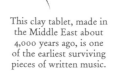

This clay tablet, made in
the Middle East about
4,000 years ago, is one
of the earliest surviving
pieces of written music.

Performing music

Any music you hear was composed by someone somewhere. But music often needs other people too, as well as people to listen to it.

Performers
play and sing the music.

A conductor
helps all the musicians to play and sing together.

Musical instruments

Some instruments associated with classical music today developed from earlier ones that changed over time as technology developed. Some surviving instruments date back thousands of years, but most are too fragile to play.

Egyptian paintings, dating back 3,000 years, show that the ancient Egyptians played a variety of pipes and stringed instruments.

This illustration comes from a German Bible made over 700 years ago. It shows King David playing a lyre, an ancestor of the harp.

This 400-year-old violin is known as a Stradivarius, after the violin-maker, Antonio Stradivari, who came from Cremona, Italy.

What did music sound like in the past?

No one can be sure exactly what music sounded like before recording was invented. The further back in time you go, the harder it is. But there are clues from books and paintings – and even early photographs – about how instruments were made and how people played and sang.

This photograph of Joachim, a famous 19th-century violinist, is one of the earliest photographs of a musician.

It shows us how he held his instrument and bow.

This painting of an early guitar player, by 17th-century Dutch artist Johannes Vermeer, helps show experts how the guitar was made, and how it was held and played.

Internet links

- Scan this code for some music to listen to.

- For more links, go to www.usborne.com/quicklinks

Writing music down

A thousand years ago, the easiest way to share music was to write it down using a system called notation. Among the first people to do this were monks, men who lived in monasteries, devoting their lives to singing and praying to God.

Monks had to sing prayers called chants six times a day. There were thousands of different tunes to learn. So they used symbols called neumes to help them remember, and wrote them down in documents called manuscripts.

High notes and low notes

An Italian monk named Guido d'Arezzo is often considered to be the inventor of modern music notation. He wrote neumes on parallel lines, so singers could see clearly how the notes went up and down.

He also invented sol-fa, a system of note names, which made it much easier to read, learn and describe music.

This manuscript shows neumes (solid black squares) on lines, with the sol-fa names in red. This is the origin of the 'do re mi' system.

A 19th-century statue of Guido d'Arezzo, who came from the town of Arezzo in Italy

How notation changed music

At first everyone sang the same tune. But notation made music so much easier to remember that people began to try singing two or more tunes at the same time. This big change, known as *polyphony* (Greek for 'many sounds'), happened in the 12th century.

Polyphony first became fashionable at Notre Dame Cathedral in Paris, which was at the heart of musical culture in the Middle Ages.

4

Notation helped music spread from monasteries and churches to the courts of kings and nobles. But because manuscripts had to be made by hand, only very rich people could afford them.

Manuscripts were often very elaborate. This heart-shaped one, made in France in the 15th century, contains the words and music for love songs.

The first printed music

In the 15th century, printing was introduced for the first time in Europe. Printing music made producing manuscripts much quicker and cheaper. Now more people could learn to sing and play, so music became a popular form of entertainment.

Ottaviano Petrucci set up a printing press in Venice, Italy, in 1501 and became one of the first people to print music.

Petrucci printed music by many composers, including this piece by Alexander Agricola.

Sharing music

Before recording was invented, print was the most popular way of sharing music for other people to play. Printed music has changed in many ways as technology has developed.

The first music was printed in black and white, but in the 19th century some began to appear with colour illustrations, like this song from the opera *Manon* by the French composer Massenet.

Today, most music notation is created by computer.

Internet links

- Scan this code for some music to listen to.
- For more links, go to www.usborne.com/quicklinks

Music and religion

Music has played a big part in religious ceremonies for thousands of years. In fact, a lot of the music that we think of as 'classical' first developed in churches and monasteries.

This lyre (small harp), made around 4,500 years ago in Mesopotamia (modern Iraq), was probably played at religious ceremonies.

Ancient Greek paintings like this one show music being played in a temple.

Statues of the ancient Egyptian cat goddess Bastet often show her holding a ceremonial rattle called a sistrum.

Gregorian chant

In the 6th century, an Italian monk named Gregorius taught singing in a slow, simple style so people could hear the words. This was known as Gregorian chant. Chanting is still important in religious music today.

Gregorius became Pope Gregory I in 590. After his death, music became more elaborate. Bigger churches were built, so larger groups of singers, called choirs, were needed to fill them with sound.

Chants – shown here in this illustrated manuscript – were among the first pieces of music to be written down. They have been sung in churches for over 1,500 years.

Russian Orthodox Church priests sing as they process around a church.

A choir singing at the church of l'Abbaye aux Dames, in Saintes, France

Part of a gospel choir from Soweto, South Africa

Playing with pipe organs

Gradually, musical instruments were added, to make church music louder and more impressive. One of the first was a pipe organ. Its powerful sound is made by pumping air with bellows through wood or metal pipes. Each pipe plays a different note, depending on its length.

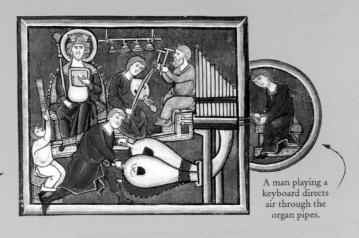

Before electricity, bellows were usually pumped by hand.

A man playing a keyboard directs air through the organ pipes.

Life as a church musician

Hundreds of years ago, churches were rich and powerful and employed thousands of musicians to write and perform music for worship. Even successful musicians, such as 16th-century Italian composer Palestrina, worked very hard for not much money.

Palestrina taught music to the choir and conducted it in church – usually three times a day.

He had to write music for religious services called masses, and for other church ceremonies as well.

He had to obey the church's strict rules about how to write music.

Two famous church composers

Here are two famous composers of religious music: one of the most famous, a German named Johann Sebastian Bach, and one of the earliest, a German nun, Hildegard of Bingen, who wrote music in the 12th century.

Hildegard founded two monasteries for women and wrote many pieces of music. This picture is from *Scivias*, a book she wrote about religion.

Born in 1685, J.S. Bach wrote hundreds of pieces of religious music – as well as music for orchestra, keyboard and solo instruments. At least four of his children became successful musicians too.

Internet links

- Scan this code for some music to listen to.
- For more links, go to www.usborne.com/quicklinks

Music for entertainment

Concerts as we know them today didn't exist before the 18th century. For most people, the only opportunity to hear musicians playing was at dances and fairs, often held near castles and palaces.

These musicians are playing early stringed instruments: two hurdy-gurdies (left) and a psaltery (right).

This picture from a 13th-century manuscript shows a troubadour named Perdigon playing a rebec, an ancestor of the violin.

All over Europe in the Middle Ages, singers moved from town to town, writing songs and performing for noblemen. The most famous of these, known as troubadours, worked in southern France, about 700 years ago.

Pons de Capduelh, shown in this painting, was a 13th-century French knight and troubadour.

A time of new ideas

In the 14th century, new ideas about learning and culture began to spread through Europe, in a period known as the Renaissance. Music was an important part of this and more and more people learned to sing and play.

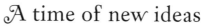

This portable keyboard instrument, called a virginal, was built to be played at home by amateur musicians.

There are two viol players in this painting by 17th-century Dutch artist Pieter Jacobsz Codde.

The man on the left is playing a lute, and the woman singing is holding a music book.

Five hundred years ago, before violins, violas, cellos and double basses, the most popular stringed instruments were viols. They came in many different sizes.

8

Marching musicians

In most places, it was rare to hear organized music in public. But in a few cities, such as Venice, processions and parades – sometimes with hundreds of marching musicians – were a part of daily life.

In the 17th century, it began to be fashionable for people to go to public ballrooms to dance and listen to music. Books were published to teach different steps and tunes.

Vauxhall Gardens, shown here in a 19th-century picture, opened in London around 1650. For 200 years it was one of London's most popular venues for dances and concerts. It attracted huge crowds of people. One ball in the 1780s was attended by more than 60,000 people.

Making music at home

Before recording was invented, the only way to hear music at home was to play it yourself. Home concerts became very fashionable in the 18th century. Pianos, flutes and violins were the most popular instruments.

18th-century British cartoonist James Gillray made fun of the fashion for home music-making. He called this picture 'The Pic-Nic Orchestra'.

Austrian composer Josef Haydn (1732-1809) wrote the first string quartets for amateur musicians. Music written for small groups, to be played in private settings, is known as chamber music.

A string quartet is a group of four instruments: two violins, a viola and a cello.

Automatic music

In the 19th century, pianos were the most popular musical instruments in Europe and the USA. Thanks to a new invention called a player piano, people could even make music if they couldn't play.

Automatic pianos were powered by foot-pedals (and later by electricity).

Internet links
- Scan this code for some music to listen to.
- For more links, go to www.usborne.com/quicklinks

Operas

At the end of the 16th century, composers began creating musical plays called operas. In an opera, actors usually sing the words instead of speaking them.

One of the first operas was *L'Orfeo*, written by Italian composer Monteverdi, based on an ancient Greek myth. It was first shown at the palace of the Duke of Mantua, in Italy, in 1607.

L'Orfeo tells the story of Orpheus, a musician whose wife, Eurydice, vanished to the underworld, the land of the dead.

Operas often involved elaborate scenery and costumes, and soon became popular all over Europe. Special opera houses were built, and some opera singers became very famous.

The Teatro San Carlo in Naples, Italy, opened in 1737 and is one of the oldest opera houses still in use today.

Opera stories

Many other early operas were based on ancient myths too. *Dido and Aeneas* by Purcell, first performed in London in 1688, is about the Queen of Carthage during the Trojan Wars.

Handel's *Giulio Cesare*, which tells the story of Julius Caesar and Cleopatra, was first performed in London in 1724.

This Roman mosaic illustrates characters from the story of Dido and Aeneas.

In his day, French singer Nourrit, shown here in Gluck's *Orfeo ed Eurydice*, was one of the most famous singers of the Paris Opera House.

In the 18th century, German composer Gluck worked in Italy, France and Austria, writing nearly 50 operas. The most famous is another version of the Orpheus story, *Orfeo ed Euridice*.

Austrian composer Mozart wrote over 20 operas. One of his most famous is *The Magic Flute*. Its cast of characters includes Papageno, a bird-catcher, Sarastro, a wizard, and the Queen of the Night – who sings some of the highest notes ever written in an opera.

These costume designs were created for performances of *The Magic Flute* in Berlin in 1816.

Papageno the bird-catcher

Sarastro, the wizard

A Russian set design for Verdi's *Otello*, based on Shakespeare's play *Othello*

Italian composer Verdi wrote about 30 operas, including some based on plays by Shakespeare. He was so popular that when he died a choir of 820 singers sang at his funeral.

The longest opera

German composer Wagner took 26 years to write *The Ring*, a series of four operas based on ancient German myths, which takes about 20 hours to perform. First staged at Bayreuth, in Germany, in 1876, it takes place around the River Rhine, featuring gods, giants, a dragon, an enchanted ring, magical beings, fires and battles.

Benjamin Britten wrote an opera called *Noye's Fludde* in the 1950s for a mixture of amateur and professional musicians, adults and children. It is based on the story of Noah's ark.

Modern operas

Today, operas are based on everything from children's books to popular culture. And they're performed not just in opera houses, but football pitches, amphitheatres and restaurants too.

Internet links

- Scan this code for some music to listen to.
- For more links, go to www.usborne.com/quicklinks

Music for ballet

Ballet, which is performed by professional dancers on stage, first developed about 400 years ago from formal dances and pageants held at French and Italian palaces.

The world's first ballet company was set up in 1661 by Louis XIV of France. He himself performed as a dancer, and employed a composer named Lully to direct the royal ballet and opera.

An outdoor ballet performance at Versailles, Louis XIV's palace, near Paris

By the 18th century, ballet wasn't just performed in palaces – but in public places too. Costumes and scenery became increasingly elaborate, and some dancers became famous.

This flamboyant 18th-century costume was designed for *Les Indes Galantes*, an opera and ballet with music by Rameau, set in exotic locations – from Persia to Peru.

Marie-Anne de Cupis, known as 'La Camargo', shown here, was the first dancer to wear a slightly shorter dress. This made jumps and leaps easier.

Some ballets use existing music. *Les Sylphides*, shown here, was first performed in 1909, to music by Chopin, who had died 70 years earlier.

Composing music for ballet

Some ballets have music written specially for them. In the 19th century, Tchaikovsky wrote some of his most famous music – *Swan Lake*, *Sleeping Beauty* and *The Nutcracker* – for shows by Russian ballet companies.

A scene from a performance of *The Nutcracker* in London in 2005

Telling stories

Like operas, early ballets were often based on Greek and Roman legends, and later on other stories too. The person who tells a story through dance steps is called a choreographer.

Tchaikovsky's *Sleeping Beauty* is based on a fairy tale by French author Charles Perrault.

Shakespeare's story *Romeo and Juliet* was turned into a ballet with music written by Russian composer Prokofiev.

The shock of the new

Ballet began to change radically in the 20th century, and one company, the *Ballets Russes*, was very controversial. When it first performed *L'Apres-midi d'un Faune* in 1912, using music by Debussy, audiences were shocked by its bizarre costumes and style of dancing.

The programme was illustrated by Russian artist Léon Bakst, who also designed the costumes and the sets.

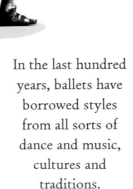

The lead dancer and choreographer, Nijinksy, shown here dressed as a faun, a half-man, half-goat from Roman mythology

A year later, the *Ballets Russes* produced *The Rite of Spring*, with music specially written for it by Russian composer Stravinsky. Today it's regarded as a masterpiece, but the first audiences found it so strange that a riot broke out and the police had to intervene.

Ravel's *Boléro*, first performed in 1928 in Paris, is based on an old Spanish dance.

In the last hundred years, ballets have borrowed styles from all sorts of dance and music, cultures and traditions.

Stravinsky's music for *Petrushka*, set in a fairground, includes Russian folk tunes.

Internet links

- Scan this code for some music to listen to.
- For more links, go to www.usborne.com/quicklinks

The Orchestra

An orchestra is a large group of musicians playing different instruments. The first classical orchestras, of up to 50 players, developed in the early 18th century. This is what an orchestra would have looked like by the end of the century.

How an orchestra works

An orchestra is made up of four main groups, or sections: strings, woodwind, brass and percussion. The colours of the stage here show you which instrument belongs to which section.

- String section
- Wind section
- Brass section
- Percussion section

Everyone who plays the same instrument sits together. Each instrument or group of instruments plays a different line of music, called a part. These parts all fit together.

Keeping it all together

In the 18th century, one musician stood in front of the orchestra to show the others when to start and stop, the speed of the music, and how loudly to play. A hundred years later, this began to be done by a separate musician, a conductor, who doesn't play an instrument.

Some conductors hold a special stick called a baton, which makes their gestures easier to see. This is American conductor Marin Alsop.

French horns

Clarinets

Flutes

First violins

Second violins

The first orchestra

The first permanent orchestra was formed around 1720 at the palace of the Elector (or governor) of Mannheim, in Germany. Soon, other European rulers wanted orchestras of their own.

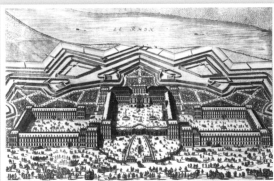

The Elector's Palace at Mannheim

In the 19th century, the number of orchestras grew, and they grew in size too. Today, orchestras can have up to 150 musicians.

A modern classical orchestra

Modern orchestras still follow the same 18th-century plan and layout, but they often include a wider variety of instruments, including a harp and percussion instruments such as marimba.

Trumpets

Timpani

Bassoons

Oboes

Violas

Cellos

Double basses

The players have their music in front of them on a music stand so they know what to play.

Playing the marimba

Internet links

- Scan this code for some music to listen to.
- For more links, go to www.usborne.com/quicklinks

Concerts

Until the late 18th century, there were hardly any public concert halls – and hardly any concerts. Any concerts that were held took place in churches, palaces and theatres.

Built in 1748, the Holywell Music Room in Oxford, England, is the oldest purpose-built concert hall in Europe.

People often moved around the room chatting and eating while the music was playing, as you can see in this 18th-century print by Thomas Rowlandson.

As orchestras became more common, concert halls were built where people went especially to listen to music. It began to be easier and cheaper to go to concerts.

Symphonies, concertos & overtures

The most popular pieces at early concerts were symphonies, concertos and overtures. They had originally been played at religious services, operas, ballets, court ceremonies and dances, but composers began to develop them for concert-hall audiences.

A concerto usually has three separate sections, called movements, with a special part for a solo instrument.

The solo player – like the violinist shown here – stands or sits at the front of the orchestra and plays the piece from memory.

Overtures were first written to start a ballet or opera, but later became pieces in their own right.

Symphonies are usually made up of four movements – often with a gap between each one.

Some of the movements in a symphony developed from old court dances, such as gavottes, minuets and jigs.

Tchaikovsky's *1812 Overture* celebrates the Russian victory over Napoleon's army at Moscow (shown here in this painting by A. F. Smirnov). It includes the sound of cannon fire.

Court musicans, like these ones in a procession in Venice, always wore a matching uniform, known as a livery.

Concert traditions

Some things about concerts haven't changed much for centuries. Early concerts had posters to advertise them, just as they do today.

This poster from 1896 announces a symphony concert in Brussels, and tells people where to buy tickets.

What happens in a concert

When the players arrive on stage, most of them sit down and adjust their instruments. This is called 'tuning up'.

Then, the most senior violinist (known as the leader or concert-master) comes on stage and takes a bow, followed by the conductor. The audience claps and the music begins.

By the time French artist Raoul Dufy painted this picture of an orchestra in 1942, concert musicians had adopted the custom of dressing all in black.

Listening to music

Mozart started performing in public as a very small child. His letters tell us he was surprised if audiences listened attentively or clapped at the end.

The idea of sitting quietly to listen didn't start until the 19th century. The composer Mahler asked audiences not to clap between the movements of some of his pieces, because he thought applause would spoil the atmosphere.

A silhouette of Gustav Mahler

Today, most people wait until the end of a piece to clap. Concert halls ask listeners to turn off their phones to avoid distracting the musicians and other listeners.

Internet links
- Scan this code for some music to listen to.
- For more links, go to www.usborne.com/quicklinks

Music and monarchy

In the past, many kings, queens and other rulers engaged musicians to work for them, and encouraged people to adopt music as a hobby. This helped make music fashionable and made many composers famous. Some monarchs were particularly known for their musical connections.

Music in Tudor England

Many European musicians worked for Henry VIII of England. The King played several instruments himself and composed music, including a song, *'Pastime with Good Company'*.

Henry VIII is shown here playing an instrument. Some people even think he wrote a popular tune called *'Greensleeves'*.

At the top of this 16th-century manuscript of the song *'Pastime with Good Company'* are the words, 'The kynge h viii'.

Queen Elizabeth I employed some of the most famous composers of the age, including William Byrd and Thomas Tallis.

This portrait of Elizabeth I playing the lute was painted by Nicholas Hilliard around 1580.

A dancing king

King Louis XIV of France was a musician and dancer. His nickname, 'the sun king' came from the costume he wore when he danced in a ballet, written by his court composer, Lully, when he was only fourteen years old.

Statue of Lully by 17th-century French sculptor Collignon

A royal challenge

In 1747, German composer J. S. Bach visited Frederick the Great at his palace in Potsdam, Germany. Frederick had recently bought a fortepiano, an early type of piano.

Frederick showed Bach a short tune he had written and asked him to continue it. So Bach wrote a set of piano pieces and musical games for him, called *The Musical Offering*.

Bach was one of the first people to play Frederick's fortepiano, which was made by a German manufacturer named Silbermann.

Royal fireworks

In 1749, Handel wrote music specially for a firework display held in London for King George II. The music was played by wind instruments, but at later performances Handel included stringed instruments too.

This old engraving shows the fireworks display on the river. The music was a great success – but a specially constructed wooden building, built to store the fireworks, burned down during the performance.

A change of heart

In 1804, when German composer Beethoven had just finished his third symphony, he dedicated it to Napoleon and wrote his name on the cover, because he admired the French military leader so much.

This painting by French artist Jacques-Louis David, showing Napoleon crossing the Alps on a fiery horse, was a piece of political propaganda. In fact he rode on a mule, led by guides.

Beethoven scratched out Napoleon's name so hard that he made a hole in the paper.

But when Napoleon declared himself 'Emperor of the French', Beethoven was so angry that he erased his name from the music and renamed the symphony *Eroica*, meaning 'heroic'.

Music and painting

Paintings often tell us about music in the past, and sometimes music tells us about pictures. Many artists loved painting musicians, and pictures often inspired composers to write music.

Musical clues

Art experts used to think this picture, *Concert in an egg*, was painted by 15th-century Dutch artist Hieronymus Bosch – until someone looked more closely at the music in the painting.

The music was written by Thomas Crecquillon, who lived years after Bosch died. Experts are still uncertain who the real artist was.

Old instruments do exist, but many are too fragile to play. To hear what they sounded like, instrument makers have to build modern copies.

Instrument makers often rely on old paintings – like this 17th-century French one of a hurdy gurdy player – to try to work out how the instrument was made.

The way instruments are played affects how they sound. Some modern musicians study paintings and copy playing styles, to find out how music might have sounded in the past.

These paintings from different centuries show how different playing positions and types of bow affect a violin's sound.

17th century

Here, the player holds his violin low against his chest, and the bow high up the stick, flat on the strings. This makes a sweet, quiet sound without much variation.

18th century

This player holds his violin under his chin, with the bow at an angle, quite high up the stick. The bow is curved outwards, with the hair quite tight. This makes a louder, clearer sound.

20th century

The player's hands and arms are higher. The bow is longer, less curved, with looser hair, held low down the stick, making it easier to control. This makes a more powerful, varied sound.

Pictures at an exhibition

When a Russian painter, Viktor Hartmann, died suddenly in 1873, aged 39, his friends organized an exhibition of his paintings. One friend, Mussorgsky, composed *Pictures at an Exhibition*, a set of piano pieces each based on one of the paintings – linked by a 'promenade' theme, to represent someone walking around the gallery.

One of the pieces, *'The Great Gate of Kiev'*, was inspired by Hartmann's design for a monumental city gate (above left).

Fifty years later, in 1922, French composer Ravel arranged the pieces for orchestra.

New art, new music

In the 20th century, some painters began using patterns and shapes, instead of images of real life, while composers began writing pieces that didn't use traditional tunes or harmonies.

Both the painting and the music shocked audiences at the time. Painters and musicians often borrowed ideas from each other.

Russian painter Kandinsky believed he could see music and hear colours. He gave musical titles to many of his paintings. This one is called *Composition VI*.

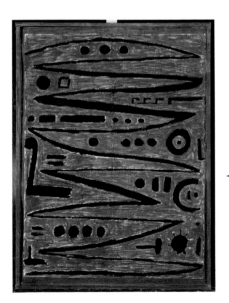

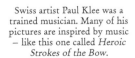

Swiss artist Paul Klee was a trained musician. Many of his pictures are inspired by music – like this one called *Heroic Strokes of the Bow*.

Internet links
- Scan this code for some music to listen to.
- For more links, go to www.usborne.com/quicklinks

Music and nature

The sights and sounds of nature have often inspired composers to write music.

'*Sumer is icumen in*' is a medieval English song. The title means '*Summer is coming*'. No one knows who composed it.

13th-century manuscript of '*Sumer is icumen in*'

'*Summer is coming*' is written for up to six people to sing at once. When the first singer reaches the red cross in the picture on the left, the second starts, and so on. This type of song is called a round.

The four seasons

One of the most famous compositions inspired by nature is *The Four Seasons*, a set of four violin concertos written in 1723 by Antonio Vivaldi, an Italian composer and violinist. The music describes things he saw and heard as the seasons changed in the countryside around Mantua, where he lived.

In Vivaldi's time, instruments were often highly decorated with scenes from nature.

Nature and emotion

In the 19th century, some composers wrote pieces expressing their feelings about nature. Beethoven, a nature lover, was one of the first to do this. He wrote his *Pastoral* symphony in 1808.

Beethoven visited the countryside as often as he could. The start of the symphony is called, '*Cheerful feelings upon arrival in the country*'.

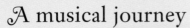

A musical landscape

In 1830, Mendelssohn left his home in Germany to visit the Hebrides islands, off the west coast of Scotland. He was so astonished by a place known as Fingal's Cave (see left) that a tune came into his head. He wrote it down and later used it for his piece *The Hebrides*.

A musical journey

Smetana, a Czech composer, wrote *Vltava*, a piece for orchestra, in 1874. It depicts the longest river in Bohemia (now the Czech Republic) as it starts in the mountains, flows through Prague, and finally joins the river Elbe.

This 19th-century painting by German artist Vincenz Morstadt shows a barge on the Vltava river in Prague.

'The Swan' was used for a ballet, first performed in 1905 by Russian dancer Anna Pavlova.

The Carnival of the Animals

In 1886 French composer Saint-Saëns wrote *The Carnival of the Animals*, a set of 14 pieces for orchestra representing different animals. The most famous section is *'The Swan'*, a beautiful tune played by a solo cello.

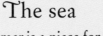

Some of the creatures who feature in *The Carnival of the Animals*

The sea

La mer is a piece for large orchestra written by French composer Claude Debussy. It is like a painting of the sea in sound.

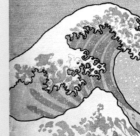

CLAUDE DEBUSSY

LA MER

Debussy was fascinated by Japanese painting. This picture by Japanese painter Hokusai appeared on the front cover of *La Mer*.

Internet links

- Scan this code for some music to listen to.
- For more links, go to www.usborne.com/quicklinks

Words and music

Some music is written especially to go with words, but at certain times the ideas of writers and poets have inspired the development of music itself.

This painting shows Dufay with a portable organ. Binchois, another composer, is holding a harp.

Religious songs were the first to be written down, with words in Latin (the language of the Church).

But, in the 15th century, composers such as Dufay (see left) began to write popular non-religious songs in their own languages.

Here is the start of his song, *'Se la face ay pale'*. The title means, 'If my face is pale'.

Dufay and others wove popular songs into their religious music too. The most famous popular song of the time was *'L'homme armé'*, or *'The armed man'*, which was used in many pieces by different composers.

'L'homme armé' also appears in two masses by Josquin des Prez, a Renaissance composer who worked in Italy.

Madrigals

A new type of song, known as a madrigal, developed in Italy in the 16th century. Madrigals were sung by several singers, sometimes with a few instruments. They were mostly about mythology, love and war. Many composers used poems by Petrarch, a 14th-century Italian.

The fashion for madrigals quickly spread to England. Thomas Morley, a composer who worked for Elizabeth I, used poems by Shakespeare as a setting for his madrigals.

Singing madrigals became a fashionable pastime for wealthy people. This 16th-century painting by Italian artist Lorenzo Costa shows two singers and a lute player.

A 19th-century book showing Morley's music for, *'It was a Lover and his Lass'* from Shakespeare's play *As you Like it*

24

A new way of thinking

In the 19th century, some German writers and artists started to explore the idea that the world was ruled by emotions and unexplained forces. This movement, known as Romanticism, soon spread and affected music too.

Many German composers, including Schubert, Schumann and Brahms, began setting Romantic poems to music, and tried to express emotions and feelings in their music.

Painted in 1818 by Caspar David Friedrich, '*The Wanderer above the Sea of Fog*' is one of the most famous Romantic paintings of the period.

For his song, '*Am Meer*', or '*By the Sea*', Schubert used a poem by Heinrich Heine, one of the best known Romantic poets.

Schubert wrote over 600 songs, as well as nine symphonies and hundreds of piano pieces.

Brahms is best known for his symphonies and piano music, but he also composed songs from Romantic poems.

Schumann wrote hundreds of songs, four symphonies, and piano pieces.

Romantic composers also tried to express emotions in music without words. Mendelssohn wrote nearly 50 piano pieces called *Songs Without Words*.

Problems of modern life

In the 20th century, many authors began to write about unhappy aspects of modern life, which influenced artists and composers too. One example was *Pierrot Lunaire*, a set of poems about Pierrot, an unhappy clown, which inspired both music and painting.

The *Pierrot Lunaire* poems were the inspiration for this painting by Swiss artist Paul Klee.

Austrian composer and painter Arnold Schoenberg used 21 of the *Pierrot Lunaire* poems for a group of songs. The music has been used many times for ballet and theatre productions.

Internet links
- Scan this code for some music to listen to.
- For more links, go to www.usborne.com/quicklinks

Music and science

Through the ages, scientists and musicians have been interested in the way sound and music work together and scientists have helped musicians in many ways.

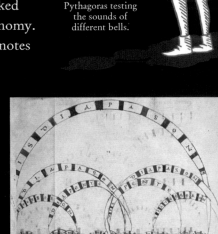

This illustration from a 15th-century book called *Theorica Musicae* shows Pythagoras testing the sounds of different bells.

The Ancient Greek philosopher Pythagoras linked music to the human body, mathematics and astronomy. He realized that bells and strings made different notes depending on their size and length.

Pythagoras's followers explored his ideas. A thousand years later, one of them, Boethius, wrote a book on music theory, *De Institutione Musica*, which was influential for the next thousand years.

This illustration of a person playing a rebec comes from a medieval copy of Boethius's book.

De Institutione Musica also describes the relationships between musical notes and how they fit together.

Music and stars and planets

Many people believed music was linked to the movement of planets. An astronomer named Kepler wrote *Harmonices Mundi* in 1619, giving each planet a musical pattern.

Saturnus   Jupiter   Mars fcrè   Terra
Venus   Mercurius   Hic locum habet etiam

A page from *Harmonices Mundi*

Herschel is famous for discovering the planet Uranus, and two of its major moons.

William Herschel was a professional violinist, organist and composer who wrote over 20 symphonies. Music inspired him to study astronomy.

Did you know?

- Gustav Holst wrote a symphony called *The Planets*, with seven pieces, one for each planet that had been discovered when he finished it in 1916. 'Neptune', the name of the most distant planet, is one of the first pieces ever written to fade slowly into silence at the end.

Music, light and colour

In the 17th century, scientist Isaac Newton studied how light splits through a prism into seven colours. He linked each one to a musical note.

Each key opened a flap to let the light through a different colour.

These are the colours Scriabin linked to each musical key.

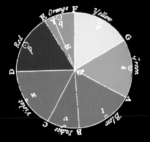

Newton's diagram of colours and notes

In France in the 1720s, Père Castel, a scientist and priest, invented a 'colour keyboard'. When the keys were pressed, it shone light through glass panels.

The composer Scriabin felt musical keys had different colours and moods. In 1910, he wrote a part for coloured lights in *Prometheus*, his fifth symphony.

Music and mathematics

Many early mathematicians studied musical tuning – the way notes are related and how instruments are adjusted. At first most instruments could only be tuned to play a few groups of notes – or keys –at once. To change the key, the instrument had to be retuned. This could take a long time.

In this 17th-century painting by Bernardo Strozzi, a man is tuning a lute by turning the pegs to change the length of the strings.

During the Renaissance, a new tuning system was developed by several people, including Vincenzo Galilei, the father of astronomer Galileo. It meant instruments could play in any of 24 keys without retuning.

Chopin

Rachmaninov

Shostakovich

Nowadays many people use electronic tuners for tuning. Before these were invented, tuning was done just by listening. Most professional musicians still tune this way.

Starting with Bach, some composers, including Chopin, Rachmaninov and Shostakovich, have challenged themselves to write sets of keyboard pieces in all 24 keys.

Internet links
- Scan this code for some music to listen to.
- For more links, go to www.usborne.com/quicklinks

Music and technology

Changes in technology over the centuries
have influenced the way music is played
and how it sounds.

A harpsichord has strings plucked by quills. From the
17th century, some harpsichords were fitted with extra
strings, controlled by two or even three keyboards.
This made them louder, with more variety of sound.

Keyboard instruments

Keyboard mechanisms were first developed in the 14th century
for clavichords and harpsichords – the ancestors of the piano –
using technology first developed by clock and watchmakers.

Cristofori's keyboard
mechanism was different
from the one used in
harpsichords.

The first pianos were invented by Bartolomeo Cristofori
in 1700. For the first time, loudness was affected by how
hard a player pressed the keys. Pianos grew bigger, louder
and more popular in the 19th century.

As well as composing piano music, Chopin and Liszt
(above) became so famous as pianists, they were
treated like stars wherever they performed.

Stringed instruments

Early stringed instruments were small and quiet. But wood-working technology and materials
improved, so people could build larger, louder ones. One of the largest is a theorbo, first
invented in the 16th century. Gradually, instrument makers built bigger and bigger ones.

These early
stringed
instruments
are called viols.
From the 17th
century, they
were gradually
replaced by
louder, more
powerful ones:
violins, violas,
cellos and
double basses.

The biggest
theorboes
today are 2m
(6 ft) long.

Wind instruments

Flutes are some of the earliest instruments ever found. Even ancient ones, made out of bones, had finger-holes for playing different notes. Later, people made longer tubes out of metal or wood with more precise holes, and flutes became very versatile and popular.

The earliest flutes, made out of hollow bird bones about 30,000 years ago, were found in Germany.

In the 16th century, keys (small tabs of leather or metal) were added to wind instruments. Keys helped players to cover the holes in different combinations. This made instruments like flutes and clarinets louder and clearer, with more notes available.

An 18th-century clarinet with holes and keys

Mozart wrote a lot of clarinet music for Anton Stadler, a famous clarinet player shown in this silhouette.

In this picture, 18th-century flute player Johann Quantz is teaching Frederick II of Prussia to play the flute. They are covering the holes with the fingers of both hands.

Brass instruments

The first brass instruments could only play a few notes. To be able to play other notes, the player had to change the length of the tube by adding or removing pieces called crooks.

In the 19th century, valves that open and close, making the tubes longer or shorter, were invented for trumpets and horns. This made it easier to play a wide variety of notes.

These are 18th-century trumpets. The one on the left has crooks attached.

Valves on a modern horn

Sound recording

Before recording, you could only hear music if someone sang or played it. The first recording machines were made in the 1870s. Recording meant music could be preserved and shared more easily.

In 1888, Emile Berliner invented a way to record and duplicate music on glass discs. This was the very start of commercial recorded music.

In Eastern Europe, composers such as Kodály and Bartók – shown in a village collecting Slovak folk songs – used wax cylinders to record traditional songs that few other people had ever heard. They later used some of this music in their own compositions.

Internet links

- Scan this code for some music to listen to.
- For more links, go to www.usborne.com/quicklinks

Timeline

Here are the dates of the lives of composers and other people mentioned in this book. (Some of the early dates are approximate.)

480 - 525	Boethius
540 - 604	Gregory I
991 - 1033	Guido d'Arezzo
1098 - 1179	Hildegard of Bingen
1190 - 1212	Perdigon
1190 - 1237	Pons de Capduelh
1397 - 1474	Dufay
1450 - 1521	Josquin
1466 - 1539	Petrucci
1491 - 1547	Henry VIII
1505 - 1557	Crecquillon
1505 - 1585	Tallis
1525 - 1594	Palestrina
1540 - 1623	Byrd
1558 - 1602	Morley
1567 - 1643	Monteverdi
1632 - 1687	Lully
1638 - 1713	Louis XIV
1659 - 1695	Purcell
1678 - 1741	Vivaldi
1683 - 1764	Rameau
1685 - 1750	Bach
1685 - 1759	Handel

About 40,000 years ago
Earliest known musical instruments.

About 4,000 years ago
Images of musical instruments appear in the art of ancient Egypt, Greece and Rome.

600 - 1100
Music develops mostly in monasteries and churches.

About 1,000 years ago
First music notation on lines.

About 900 years ago
The modern pipe organ develops.

About 800 years ago
Troubadours sing at palaces.

About 700 years ago
Some composers weave popular songs into church music.

The Renaissance
Music becomes a very popular pastime.

500 years ago
Music printing develops in Venice, Italy.

Around 1550
The violin is invented in Italy.

Around 1600
The first operas are performed in Italy.

1640s
Operas and ballets are performed at the court of French King Louis XIV.

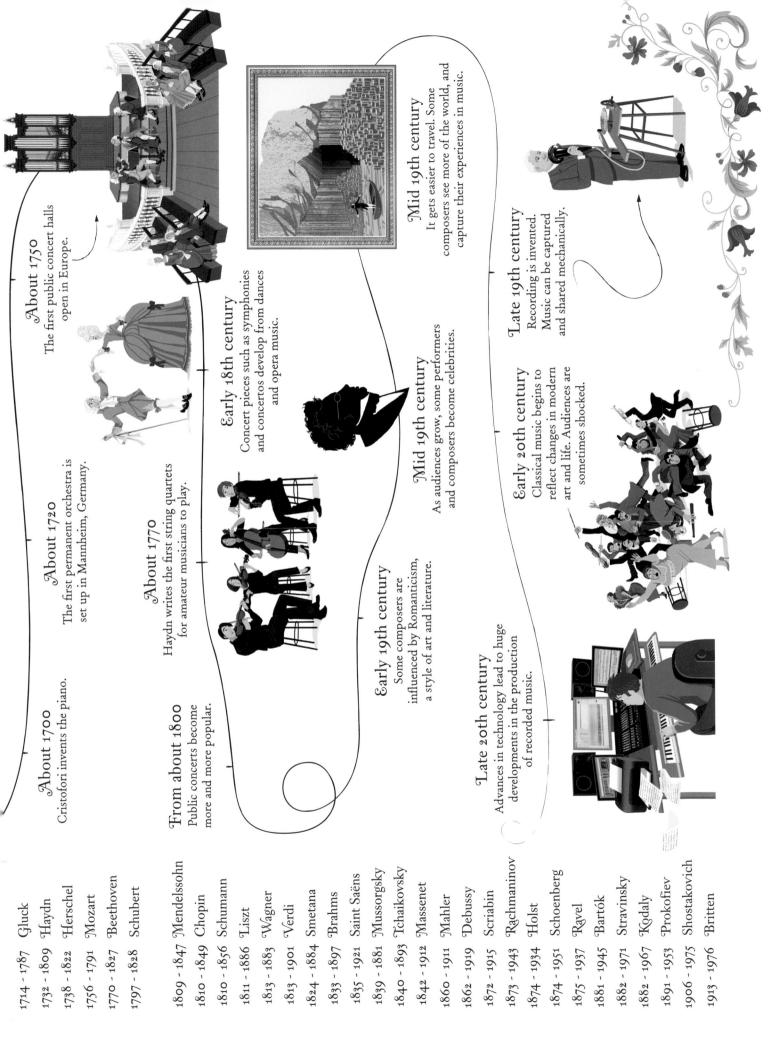

About 1750
The first public concert halls open in Europe.

About 1720
The first permanent orchestra is set up in Mannheim, Germany.

About 1700
Cristofori invents the piano.

About 1770
Haydn writes the first string quartets for amateur musicians to play.

From about 1800
Public concerts become more and more popular.

Early 18th century
Concert pieces such as symphonies and concertos develop from dances and opera music.

Early 19th century
Some composers are influenced by Romanticism, a style of art and literature.

Mid 19th century
It gets easier to travel. Some composers see more of the world, and capture their experiences in music.

Mid 19th century
As audiences grow, some performers and composers become celebrities.

Late 19th century
Recording is invented. Music can be captured and shared mechanically.

Early 20th century
Classical music begins to reflect changes in modern art and life. Audiences are sometimes shocked.

Late 20th century
Advances in technology lead to huge developments in the production of recorded music.

1714 - 1787	Gluck
1732 - 1809	Haydn
1738 - 1822	Herschel
1756 - 1791	Mozart
1770 - 1827	Beethoven
1797 - 1828	Schubert
1809 - 1847	Mendelssohn
1810 - 1849	Chopin
1810 - 1856	Schumann
1811 - 1886	Liszt
1813 - 1883	Wagner
1813 - 1901	Verdi
1824 - 1884	Smetana
1833 - 1897	Brahms
1835 - 1921	Saint Saëns
1839 - 1881	Mussorgsky
1840 - 1893	Tchaikovsky
1842 - 1912	Massenet
1860 - 1911	Mahler
1862 - 1919	Debussy
1872 - 1915	Scriabin
1873 - 1943	Rachmaninov
1874 - 1934	Holst
1874 - 1951	Schoenberg
1875 - 1937	Ravel
1881 - 1945	Bartók
1882 - 1971	Stravinsky
1882 - 1967	Kodaly
1891 - 1953	Prokofiev
1906 - 1975	Shostakovich
1913 - 1976	Britten

Index

QR codes and internet links

To hear the music samples for this book, you can scan the QR codes with a smartphone or tablet, or you can go to the Usborne Quicklinks website at www.usborne.com/quicklinks and type in the title of this book. There you'll find links to click on to hear the music samples, as well as links to websites to find out more about classical music.

Scanning the QR codes

You need a smartphone or tablet with a free app called a "QR reader" that you can download from your device's app store. Just point the device's camera at a QR code and follow your QR reader's instructions to scan the code.

Please read our internet safety guidelines at the Usborne Quicklinks website or for more advice on using the internet and scanning QR codes, see the "Help and advice" area at the Usborne Quicklinks website.

Acknowledgements

© **akg-images** *p.25* bl, *p.28* bl; © **The Bridgeman Art Library** *Cover* bm English Heritage Photo Library, *p.3* bl English Heritage Photo, *p.4* bl Alinari, Bath and North East Somerset Council, *p.6* tr Giraudon, *p.7* bl Werner Forman Archive, br Private Collection, *p.9* m Courtesy of the Warden and Scholars of New College, Oxford, *p.10* tl De Agostini Picture Library, bl Somerset County Museum, Taunton Castle, *p.11* tr Stage design for Giuseppe Verdi's opera 'Otello', by Valery Jakovelevich Levental c.1981 (oil on canvas)/Tretyakov Gallery, Moscow, Russia, By kind permission © Valery Jakovelevich Levental, *p.12* ml Private Collection/The Stapleton Collection, bl Les Sylphides (oil on canvas), Knight, Laura (1877-1970)/Birmingham Museums and Art Gallery, © Reproduced with permission of The Estate of Dame Laura Knight DBE RA 2014. All Rights Reserved, *p.16* tl Victoria Art Gallery, *p.17* tr Private Collection/The Stapleton Collection, mr The Orchestra, 1942 (oil on canvas), Dufy, Raoul (1877-1953)/Bridgestone Museum of Art, Tokyo, Japan / Giraudon, © ADAGP, Paris and DACS, London 2015., *p.18* mr, bl Giraudon, *p.19* mr Private Collection, bl, *p.20* t Giraudon, ml Private Collection, bl National Museum, Stockholm, Sweden, bm Giraudon, br Private Collection, *p.21* t Private Collection/RIA Novosti, bl Museum of Modern Art, New York, USA/Photo © Boltin Picture Library, br Composition No. 6, 1913, Kandinsky, Wassily (1866-1944)/Hermitage, St. Petersburg, Russia, *p.22* tl British Library Board. All Rights Reserved, bl 2014 Museum of Fine Arts, Boston. All rights reserved, br, *p.23* ml Private Collection/The Stapleton Collection, *p.24* tl Giraudon, mr Universal History Archive/UIG, bl National Gallery, London, UK, br Private Collection, Prismatic Pictures, *p.25* t, *p.26* bl Universal History Archive/UIG, *p.27* m De Agostini Picture Library/G.Nimatallah, *p.28* tr Giuseppe Verdi Conservatory. Italy, Photo Tarker, *p.29* m Private Collection/The Stapleton Collection; © **The British Library Board** *p.3* m Shelf Harley MS 2804, f. 3v, *p.7* tr De Agostini 87017769, *p.18* tm Shelf mark Royal 2 A. XVI, f.63v, ml Shelf mark Add. 31922, ff.14v-15, *p.24* br De Agostini 96000390; © **The Trustees of the British Museum** *p.6* tl; © **Corbis** *p.13* tr Lebrecht Music & Arts; © **Getty Images** *p.2* t&m Superstock, *p.9* bl C Squared Studios/Photodisc, *p.23* tr DEA A. Dagli Orti/De Agostini, *p.28* ml DEA L.de Masi/De Agostini; © **Herzog August Bibliothek Wolfenbüttel**:Cod. Guelf.287 Extrav.,ff, 40v-41r – detail *p.24* tr, © **Lebrecht Music and Arts** *Cover* br, *p.3* br, *p.5* bl, bm De Agostini, *p.6* br Michael Garnier, *p.9* tl De Agostini, *p.10* br Private Collection, *p.11* tl De Agostini, tm, *p.12* tr, br © Dee Conway, *p.13* ml © De Agostini, mr, bl, br © Fondation Théodore Strawinsky, *p.14* bl © T. Martinot, *p.15* mr © Michel Garnier, br © Wladimir Polak, *p.16* mr © Chris Stock, br © culture-images, *p.17* tl © De Agostini, *p.19* bm, *p.25* tr, *p.27* tr © Anne-Katrin Purkiss, bl, br, *p.28* mr, *p.29* tl © Royal Academy of Music College, tm © Chris Stock, tr © Culture images, mr © Chris Stock, bl; © **Oxford University Image Library** *p.3* mr Ashmolean Museum - All rights reserved; **Andrew Parker** *p.4* m Neume notation thanks to Andrew Parker, Ferndown, Dorset, **The Pasternak Trust** *p27* bm Portrait of Sergei Vasilievich Rachmaninov (1873-1943) at the Piano, 1916 (pastel on paper), Pasternak, Leonid Osipovic (1862-1945), reproduced by kind permission, **RMN** *p.5* tr Chanson "J'ay pris amours" and L'Amour et la Fortune Recueil: ROTHSCHILD 2973 Folio 23v, Anonyme Localisation: Paris, Bibliothèque Nationale de France (BnF) © BnF, Dist. RMN-Grand Palais / image BnF; © **Photo Scala, Florence** *Cover* bl, *p.2* t, *p.8* tl White Images, ml The Metropolitan Museum of Art/Art Resource, br, *p.17* bl, *p.26* ml © DeAgostini Picture Library; **The Schøyen Collection** *p.2* br MS 5105/www.schoyencollection.com; **State Library of Victoria Collection** *p.26* mr RARESF 091 B63; © **Topfoto** *p.8* mr Print Collector, *p.15* tr Ullsteinbild; © **Robert Workman** *p.11* bl; © **Victoria and Albert Museum, London** *p.6* ml.

Musical consultant: Rebecca Herman   Edited by Jane Chisholm